THE QUOTED LIFE

223 Best Inspirational and Motivational Quotes on Success, Mindset, Confidence, Learning, Persistence, Motivation, And Happiness

SOM BATHLA
www.sombathla.com

The Quoted Life

Your Free Gift Bundle

As a token of my thanks for taking out time to read my book, I would like to offer you a gift pack:

Click and Download your Free Gift Bundle Below

Get Your Gift Bundle!

THREE KILLER BOOKS for FREE on:
1. Mind Hacking - in just 21 days!
2. Time Hacking - How to Cheat Time!
3. The Productivity Manifesto

&

TWO FREE VIDEOS to Understand Procrastinator's Mind and How to Use Procrastination for your Benefit

Click Here To GET INSTANT ACCESS

You can also grab your FREE GIFT BUNDLE through this below URL: http://sombathla.com/freegiftbundle

More Books by Som Bathla

WHAT IF I FAIL?: Leverage your Fear of Failure & Turn into Fuel for Success, Rewire your Belief System, Learn to Trigger Action despite being Scared and Take Charge of Your Life

THE MINDSET MAKEOVER: Transform Your Mindset to Attract Success, Unleash Your True Potential, Control Thoughts and Emotions, Become Unstoppable and Achieve Your Goals Faster

The Quoted Life

Living Beyond Self Doubt: Reprogram Your Insecure Mindset, Reduce Stress and Anxiety, Boost Your Confidence, Take Massive Action despite Being Scared & Reclaim Your Dream Life

FOCUS MASTERY: Master Your Attention, Ignore Distractions, Make Better Decisions Faster and Accelerate Your Success

The Quoted Life

JUST GET IT DONE: Conquer Procrastination, Eliminate Distractions, Boost Your Focus, Take Massive Action Proactively and Get Difficult Things Done Faster

Master Your Day- Design Your Life: Develop Growth Mindset, Build Routines to Level-Up your Day, Deal Smartly with Outside World and Craft Your Dream Life

The Quoted Life

The 30 Hour Day: Develop Achiever's Mindset and Habits, Work Smarter and Still Create Time For Things That Matter

For More details and subscribing to the newsletter, please visit www.sombathla.com

The Quoted Life

TABLE OF CONTENTS:

Your Free Gift Bundle	2
More Books by Som Bathla	3
Importance of Inspirational Quotes in Life:	8
I. Quotes for achieving Success:	18
II. Quotes on Power of Mindset and Belief System:	28
III. Quotes for building more Confidence:	36
IV. Quotes on the Importance of Continuous Learning:	45
V. Quotes on significance of Persistence:	48
VI. Quotes on Motivation:	51
VII. Quotes on Happiness:	53
Thank You!	56
About the Author	58

Importance of Inspirational Quotes in Life:

- I cannot do this.
- I do not have that kind of money or time to pursue my dreams.
- I am not that smart or gifted to pursue my dreams.
- How can I ignore this depressing economy and waste my efforts in pursuing my distant dreams?

How many times have you heard about these self-sabotaging statements in your waking life? I am sure that most of us keep on playing these mental records in our heads quite frequently when we think of our dreams. It is not that we don't know the importance of the positive thinking, of being authentic, of developing courage, etc. to achieve success. But probably all our knowledge is at the surface level of our mind. In the core depth of our subconscious mind, we have strongly rooted beliefs, which allow such kind of negative thoughts to pop-up at times.

We all should be empathetic to each other because these thoughts are not solely our fault (but there is some action needed on our part, which I will cover later in this section).

The Quoted Life

The problem is that these negative statements are so frequently re-enforced through our outside environment and after that, we play it so regularly in our heads that these start appearing true. Our environment includes lots of factors like our childhood, belief systems and outlook of our parents, teachers, siblings and friends, our work environment and routine interactions with the people around.

The biggest problem with such statements is that with continuous repetitions, these statements get reinforced and solidify a negative belief system.

In my other book *"The 30 Hour Day- Develop Achiever's Mindset and Habits, Work Smarter and Still Create Time For Things That Matter"*, I have written a complete chapter on seven negative mindsets, which cripple us and how we can replace these with a positive mindset.

Also, you already know that most of the successful people have already faced the criticism from the people around them with similar kind of statements. But they chose not to consider these external talks or inner self-talks seriously. They did not allow the negativity to enter into their minds and finally, they succeeded.

- Take the example of Michael Jordan. He was removed from the high school basketball team, not being worthy to play. But he never admitted his defeat. He locked himself for the hardest training on the basketball, kept trying and today, he has millions of raving fans. He survived all adversities and consistently moved ahead in spite of the negative beliefs of people. Today his biography on the National Basketball Association (NBA) website states: *"By acclamation, Michael Jordan is the greatest basketball player of all time."*

- Thomas Edison was told by his teachers in his school days that he was too stupid to learn anything. But he didn't listen to them and persisted in his endeavors and holds more than 1000 US Patents in his name. His mantra is *"Genius is one percent inspiration, ninety-nine percent perspiration."*

- Walt Disney got fired from his newspaper agency on the ground that he lacks imagination and doesn't have original ideas. Who doesn't know him today for his widely acclaimed creative ideas and imagination for creative world famous innovations in animation and theme park designs?

The history is full of such individuals, who had seen dark times in their lives. But they conquered over their negative belief system and the criticism from the world, and finally rose as super-stars of life. The moot point is that once you are determined to do something with full dedication and intention, then the universe joins you to make that thing happen.

But in spite of wisdom available to all of us in the forms of books, literature, why doesn't one starts taking action?

The Quoted Life

One of the main reasons is fear. Fear could be of any sort, not the fear of being physically hurt only, but any intangible fear. It can be the fear of what people would say, the fear of the negative outcome, i.e., failure, the fear of criticism, the fear of self-doubt, the fear of lack of self-worth. So what is the solution?

Jim Rohn's below quote answers:

"Motivation is what gets you started. Habit is what keeps you going."- Jim Rohn

Yes, motivation plays an important role to kick-start you to take action. Once started, you have to keep taking action towards your goals, and with that enough consistency, you will soon be progressing faster.

The best way to find motivation is to follow the successful people. These people have encapsulated their wisdom nuggets gained through the lifelong experience in the form of *inspirational quotes.* These Inspirational quotes have the unique power to provide you a way forward and actionable intelligence. Also, you will find better clarity and direction in life through these quotes.

What is the Significance of Quotations?

Quotations are the life lessons stated in brief phrases by successful people. These quotes get generated from the wisdom attained by them through their lifetime of experience with blood and sweat, and who wanted others to get benefitted from their wisdom.

It is a natural tendency of human being that once he learns the wisdom of life, he can't hold it to himself/herself only. He gets deeply inspired to share

The Quoted Life

that wisdom with the world that comes out in the form of quotes, books, audio/video interviews.

Life is too short, and it is also an expensive deal to learn all the lessons from our own mistakes. Therefore, we should learn from others' mistake, which will help us to avoid falling into the trap of the similar mistakes. Following the wisdom of other successful people, will make our journey towards success shorter and less cumbersome.

There are few reasons, why quotes are helpful to lead us to ultimate success in life, developing resourceful mindsets and improving confidence in our lives.

1. **Originated from our Role Models:** The quotes are not merely regular talks from our neighborhood, surroundings, etc., rather these are generated from the people, whom we admire and follow them as our role models. That is the reason why such quotes get deeper into our mind and affect our thinking at a deeper level.

2. **We can relate ourselves:** Depending upon which phase of our lives, we are going through, we can easily relate ourselves with the quotes from these successful personalities. If we can relate our circumstances or life situation with those of our role models, it makes our journey smoother and predictable to some extent, and it improves our confidence.

3. **Consistent Reminder of what is possible:** The quotes do remind us as to what could be possible

if we just keep moving while staying focused on our goals.

4. **Helps instantly encounter negative feeling:** Once you are careful about thoughts coming to your mind on a regular basis and imbibe the quotes in your lives, it becomes very easy to counter any negative feeling generated from outside circumstances or inner negative emotions. Quotes help us to look at the brighter side of the problem and thus overcome the negativity around us.

5. **Daily Mental Spark:** During our entire day, we get encountered with all kind of people, negative news, ever distracting social media tools that trigger negative emotions in our minds. Unless we spark our mind with something positive on a regular basis, these negative thoughts have the progress to halt our progress. The quotes give us the necessary daily spark and dilute the impact of such negativity around.

6. **Creation of new belief system:** Your mind is pre-conditioned with the same set of thoughts and beliefs, as of your surrounding environment. Unfortunately, in most of the cases, one is bombarded with self-limiting beliefs that it requires the conscious effort to put positive thoughts in your mind. These quotes catalyze to replace the negative thoughts with positive beliefs that help to take the required action towards our goals.

The Quoted Life

7. **A new perspective to see the world:** imbibing of these quotes in your belief system will gradually change your mindset, and you would start seeing the world with a positive outlook. With a regular perusal of these motivational quotes, we can reassure ourselves that there are ample opportunities in life if we just start looking at the brighter side of the things. The inspirational quotes invariably help by changing our focus from the problem to the solution, from the questions to the answers.

What is "Quoted Life"

You could understand this and give it two different meanings (both are right and in fact inter-connected).

The first meaning is that once you get these resourceful quotes imbibed in your belief system, it dusts away all the negative emotions from your life. With all the positive thoughts, you can move faster towards your goals.

The other meaning and of course, this will be the natural outcome, if you have lived the first meaning. No one can stop the fragrance of a flower from spreading in the environment. Similarly, once you follow the right practices in your day to day life in a consistent manner, the others around you will ultimately get impacted, and they will start *quoting* you. So this is the advanced form of the *'The Quoted Life."*

The Quoted Life

How is this book different?

This book is divided into various sections focusing on different needs of the reader at any specific point in time. If one is focused on quotes related to succeeding in some specific area, then quotes on success will serve the purpose. However, if one needs some quotes on mindset or beliefs or significance of confidence in our lives, then such quotes can be directly located in a different section. So instead of mixing all quotes at one place, this book captures the quotes in separate categories.

This book is structured in such a manner that it caters to the needs of the reader as per their specific needs.

What is the Author's personal experience of imbibing quotes in daily life?

I love to collect the wonderful inspiration quotes spread across the internet and love to share such quotes with others.

I have personally found that when you are coming across any negative situation in your life, then such quotes help you face the tough times. Moreover, if you make a habit of incorporating selected inspirational quotes as part of your daily affirmations, then you feel more and more insulated from all the negativity in your surroundings.

These inspirational quotes have helped me in developing a resilient mindset and coping up with challenging situations. Of course, you will still come across fears of all sorts, but you will realize that the positive quotes help you sail through the difficult times

The Quoted Life

with courage. You develop your courage and stand tall in front of those fears and still take consistent actions towards your goals.

How to get the maximum benefit out of these inspirational quotes?

'Knowing is not enough, we must apply. Willing is not enough; we must do.'- Bruce Lee

If one is sincere about one's success, then the actions need to be changed. We all know that our actions are controlled by our emotions/feelings at any specific point in time. If we are feeling better, then we will take faster actions and progress better. However, if we don't feel good about anything, then we will be in the mode of procrastination and won't move further towards the actions.

Again going back still some more, it is important to remember that all our positive/negative emotions are then controlled by our thoughts from moment to moment. The thoughts running through our minds determine the quality of emotions that we feel in our hearts.

The starting point for any action is to control your thought process at the deeper level. Therefore, the next relevant question arises is how to manage our thoughts at different points of time. As Earl Nightingale has rightly quoted:

"Whatever we plant in our subconscious mind and nourish with repetition and emotion will one day become a reality." - Earl Nightingale

The Quoted Life

Therefore, you need to have a daily dose of these mental dietary supplements available in the form of these inspirational quotes.

Here is how can you use these quotes.

- Make a habit of reading daily a few quotes, depending on what mental situation you are going through that day.

- You may also shortlist few quotes and paste it in front of your desk or at a place where you can see them regularly.

- The best thing is to make it a part of your daily morning affirmations. If you want to know more about affirmations and how to use affirmation in a modern and most effective manner, you may find this in my another book *"The 30 Hour Day- Develop Achiever's Mindset and Habits, Work Smarter and Still Create Time For Things That Matter"*.

With that, I present to you the compilation of quotes in the coming section.

The Quoted Life

I. **Quotes for achieving Success:**

1. Success is peace of mind which is a direct result of self-satisfaction in knowing you did your best to become the best you are capable of becoming.- **John Wooden**

2. There are no secrets to success. It is the result of preparation, hard work, and learning from failure. – **Colin Powell**

3. I've missed more than 9,000 shots in my career. I've lost almost 300 games. 26 times, I've been trusted to take the game-winning shot and missed. I've failed over and over and over again in my life. And that is why I succeed. -**Michael Jordan**

4. "Successful people do what unsuccessful people are not willing to do. Don't wish it were easier; wish you were better." **Jim Rohn**

The Quoted Life

5. What you get by achieving your goals is not as important as what you become by achieving your goals. ~ **Henry David Thoreau**

6. In order to succeed, your desire for success should be greater than your fear of failure. – **Bill Cosby**

7. Formula for success: rise early, work hard, strike oil. –**J. Paul Getty**

8. "I have not failed. I've just found 10,000 ways that won't work." **Thomas Edison**

9. "Success is the sum of small efforts, repeated day in and day out." **Robert Collier**

10. "There is nothing to fear, because you cannot fail – only LEARN, GROW, and become BETTER than you've ever been before." – **Hal Elrod**

11. It's how you deal with failure that determines how you achieve success. – **Charlotte Whitton**

12. "Success is walking from failure to failure with no loss of enthusiasm." **Winston Churchill**

The Quoted Life

13. "The successful warrior is the average man, with laser-like focus." **Bruce Lee**

14. Success is a journey, not a destination. The doing is often more important than the outcome." – **Arthur Ashe**

15. "Whenever you find yourself on the side of the majority, it is time to pause and reflect." **Mark Twain**

16. Strength does not come from physical capacity. It comes from an indomitable will." -**Mahatma Gandhi**

17. "If you set your goals ridiculously high and it's a failure, you will fail above everyone else's success." **James Cameron**

18. "The distance between insanity and genius is measured only by success." **Bruce Feirstein**

19. "There are two types of people who will tell you that you cannot make a difference in this world: those who are afraid to try and those who are afraid you will succeed." **Ray Goforth**

The Quoted Life

20. "Whenever you see a successful person, you only see the public glories, never the private sacrifices to reach them." **Vaibhav Shah**

21. "Our greatest fear should not be of failure ... but of succeeding at things in life that don't really matter." **Francis Chan**

22. "Try not to become a person of success, but rather try to become a person of value." **Albert Einstein**

23. "All progress takes place outside the comfort zone." **Michael John Bobak**

24. "Dream Big. Start small. Act now." - **Robin Sharma**

25. "Success does not consist in never making mistakes, but in never making the same one a second time." **George Bernard Shaw**

26. "Successful and unsuccessful people do not vary greatly in their abilities. They vary in their desires to reach their potential." **John Maxwell**

The Quoted Life

27. "You may only succeed if you desire succeeding; you may only fail if you do not mind failing." **Philippos**

28. "I don't want to get to the end of my life and find that I lived just the length of it. I want to have lived the width of it as well." **Diane Ackerman**

29. "Keep on going, and the chances are that you will stumble on something, perhaps when you are least expecting it. I have never heard of anyone ever stumbling on something sitting down." **Charles F. Kettering**

30. "Would you like me to give you a formula for success? It's quite simple, really: Double your rate of failure. You are thinking of failure as the enemy of success. But it isn't at all. You can be discouraged by failure or you can learn from it, so go ahead and make mistakes. Make all you can. Because remember that's where you will find success." **Thomas J. Watson**

31. If you would hit the mark, you must aim a little above it; every arrow that flies feels the attraction of earth."– **Henry Wadsworth Longfellow**

The Quoted Life

32. "Always bear in mind that your own resolution to success is more important than any other one thing." **Abraham Lincoln**

33. "I don't know the key to success, but the key to failure is trying to please everyone**." Bill Cosby**

34. "If you genuinely want something, don't wait for it--teach yourself to be impatient." **Gurbaksh Chahal**

35. Develop success from failures. Discouragement and failure are two of the surest stepping stones to success. ~**Dale Carnegie**

36. "Don't be afraid to give up the good to go for the great." **John D. Rockefeller**

37. Don't let the fear of losing be greater than the excitement of winning. ~**Robert Kiyosaki**

38. "The successful warrior is the average man, with laser-like focus." -**Bruce Lee**

39. Success is not to be pursued; it is to be attracted by the person we become." — **Jim Rohn**

The Quoted Life

40. You may be disappointed if you fail, but you are doomed if you don't try." — **Beverly Sills**

41. "Would you like me to give you a formula for success? It's quite simple, really: Double your rate of failure. You are thinking of failure as the enemy of success. But it isn't at all. You can be discouraged by failure or you can learn from it, so go ahead and make mistakes. Make all you can. Because remember, that's where you will find success." **Thomas J. Watson**

42. I haven't failed. I've just found 10,000 ways that won't work. -**Thomas Edison**

43. When you want to succeed as bad as you want to breathe then you will be successful." -**Eric Thomas**

44. "Start where you are. Use what you have. Do what you can." **Arthur Ashe**

45. "A successful man is one who can lay a firm foundation with the bricks others have thrown at him." **David Brinkley**

46. "I find that the harder I work, the more luck I seem to have." **Thomas Jefferson**

The Quoted Life

47. For true success ask yourself these four questions: Why? Why not? Why not me? Why not now?" — **James Allen**

48. I attribute my success to this: I never gave or took any excuse. –**Florence Nightingale**

49. You miss 100% of the shots you don't take. – **Wayne Gretzky**

50. I didn't fail the test. I just found 100 ways to do it wrong. –**Benjamin Franklin**

51. Obstacles are those frightful things you see when you take your eyes off the goal. –**Henry Ford.**

52. "The whole secret of a successful life is to find out what is one's destiny to do, and then do it." **Henry Ford**

53. "Though no one can go back and make a brand-new start, anyone can start from now and make a brand-new ending." **Carl Bard**

The Quoted Life

54. "If you want to achieve excellence, you can get there today. As of this second, quit doing less-than-excellent work." **Thomas J. Watson**

55. "Small daily – seemingly insignificant – improvements and innovations lead to staggering achievements over time." - **Robin Sharma**

56. Success and failure. We think of them as opposites, but they're really not. They're companions – the hero and the sidekick." — **Laurence Shames**

57. There are so many ways to fail but only one way to succeed; NEVER GIVE UP!" — **Johni Pangalila**

58. Failure is the opportunity to begin again more intelligently." –**Henry Ford**

59. "If you want to make your dreams come true, the first thing you have to do is wake up." -**J.M. Power**

60. "Things work out best for those who make the best of how things work out." **John Wooden**

The Quoted Life

61. "The best revenge is a massive success." **Frank Sinatra**

62. "The only place where success comes before work is in the dictionary." **Vidal Sassoon**

63. "We all die. The goal isn't to live forever. The goal is to create something that will." -**Chuck Palahniuk**

64. Success demands singleness of purpose- **Vince Lombardi**

II. **Quotes on Power of Mindset and Belief System:**

65. You have to work hard to get your thinking clean to make it simple. But it's worth it in the end because once you get there; you can move mountains – **Steve Jobs.**

66. Always bear in mind that your own resolution to succeed is more important than any other." – **Abraham Lincoln**

67. "They say misery loves company, but so does mediocrity. Don't let the limiting beliefs of OTHERS limit what's possible for YOU."- **Hal Elrod**

68. Success is a state of mind. If you want success, start thinking of yourself as a success." — **Dr. Joyce Brothers**

The Quoted Life

69. "If you want to make a permanent change, stop focusing on the size of your problems and start focusing on the size of you!" **T. Harv Eker**

70. The barrier between success is not something which exists in the real world: it is composed purely and simply of doubts about ability. ~ **Franklin D. Roosevelt**

71. The only place where your dream becomes impossible is in your own thinking. – **Robert H. Schuller**

72. "You must establish and maintain the beliefs that you are capable, committed, and destined to achieve your goals." – **Hal Elrod**

73. The most common way people give up their power is by thinking they don't have any. –**Alice Walker**

74. Very often a change of self is needed more than a change of scene. ~ **Arthur Christopher Benson**

75. The starting point of all achievement & success is desire. Weak desire brings weak results. ~ **Napoleon Hill**

The Quoted Life

76. "Great minds discuss ideas; average minds discuss events; small minds discuss people." **Eleanor Roosevelt**

77. "The secret to genius is not genetics but daily practice married with relentless perseverance." - **Robin Sharma**

78. "We become what we think about most of the time, and that's the strangest secret." **Earl Nightingale**

79. "The first step toward success is taken when you refuse to be a captive of the environment in which you first find yourself." **Mark Caine**

80. "Whenever you find yourself on the side of the majority, it is time to pause and reflect." **Mark Twain**

81. "Desire is the starting point of all achievement, not a hope, not a wish, but a keen pulsating desire which transcends everything." -**Napoleon Hill**

82. Real difficulties can be overcome; it is only the imaginary ones that are unconquerable. ~**Theodore N. Vail**

The Quoted Life

83. Don't wish it was easier, wish you were better. Don't wish for less problems, wish for more skills. Don't wish for less challenge, wish for more wisdom- **Jim Rohn**

84. Ideas can be life-changing. Sometimes all you need to open the door is just one more good idea. ~ **Jim Rohn**

85. "I am who I am today because of the choices I made yesterday." -**Eleanor Roosevelt**

86. "If you start to think the problem is 'out there,' stop yourself. That thought is the problem." **Stephen Covey**

87. Whatever the mind of man can conceive and believe, it can achieve. –**Napoleon Hill**

88. "The first step toward success is taken when you refuse to be a captive of the environment in which you first find yourself." -**Mark Caine**

89. The only person you are destined to become is the person you decide to be. –**Ralph Waldo Emerson**

The Quoted Life

90. "Where you are is a result of who you were, but where you go depends entirely on who you choose to be."- **Hal Elrod**

91. Believe you can and you're halfway there. – **Theodore Roosevelt**

92. Change your thoughts and you change your world. –**Norman Vincent Peale**

93. "You see things; and you say, 'Why?' But I dream things that never were; and I say, 'Why not?'" – **George Bernard Shaw**

94. "No one can make you feel inferior without your consent." **Eleanor Roosevelt**

95. "Nobody ever wrote down a plan to be broke, fat, lazy, or stupid. Those things are what happen when you don't have a plan." **Larry Winget**

96. You will be a failure, until you impress the subconscious with the conviction you are a success. This is done by making an affirmation which clicks." – **Florence Scovel Shinn**

The Quoted Life

97. Accept responsibility for your life. Know that it is you who will get you where you want to go, no one else." -**Les Brown**

98. "You must allow yourself to start thinking BIGGER and acting BOLDER with regards to what's possible for you. Seriously. Don't wait. Start now."- **Hal Elrod**

99. "No one can make you feel inferior without your consent." **Eleanor Roosevelt**

100. We cannot solve our problems with the same thinking we used when we created them. ~ **Albert Einstein**

101. "If you can't explain it simply, you don't understand it well enough." **Albert Einstein**

102. "If you think you can, you can. And if you think you can't, you're right." – **Henry Ford**

103. "If you don't design your own life plan, chances are you'll fall into someone else's plan. And guess what they have planned for you? Not much." **Jim Rohn**

The Quoted Life

104. "Your daily behavior reveals your deepest beliefs."
 - **Robin Sharma**

105. "The No. 1 reason people fail in life is because they listen to their friends, family, and neighbors."
Napoleon Hill

106. Every achiever I have ever met says, 'My life turned around when I began to believe in me.'" – **Robert Schuller**

107. The key question to keep asking is, Are you spending your time on the right things? Because time is all you have." -**Randy Pausch**

108. "Your chances of success in any undertaking can always be measured by your belief in yourself." — **Robert Collier**

109. "It is our darkest moments that we must focus on the light." -**Aristotle Onassis**

110. "If you always put limits on everything you do, physical or anything else, it will spread into your work and into your life. There are no limits. There are only plateaus, and you must not stay there, you must go beyond them." -**Bruce Lee**

The Quoted Life

III. Quotes for building more Confidence:

111. "To be yourself in a world that is constantly trying to make you something else is the greatest accomplishment." **Ralph Waldo Emerson**

112. "If you are insecure, guess what? The rest of the world is too. Do not overestimate the competition and underestimate yourself. You are better than you think." **T. Harv Eker**

113. "Our deepest fear is not that we are inadequate. Our deepest fear is that we are powerful beyond measure. It is our light, not our darkness that most frighten us. We ask ourselves, 'Who am I to be brilliant, gorgeous, talented, fabulous?' Actually, who are you not to be?" **Marianne Williamson**

114. "Confidence is a habit that can be developed by acting as if you already had the confidence you desire to have." **Brian Tracy**

The Quoted Life

115. "To double your income, triple your investment in self-development." - **Robin Sharma**

116. "Inaction breeds doubt and fear. Action breeds confidence and courage. If you want to conquer fear, do not sit home and think about it. Go out and get busy." **Dale Carnegie**

117. "The moment you take responsibility for everything in your life is the moment you can change anything in your life." – **Hal Elrod**

118. "The way to develop self-confidence is to do the thing you fear and get a record of successful experiences behind you." **William Jennings Bryan**

119. "Talk to yourself like you would to someone you love." **Brené Brown**

120. "Low self-confidence isn't a life sentence. Self-confidence can be learned, practiced, and mastered--just like any other skill. Once you master it, everything in your life will change for the better." **Barrie Davenport**

121. "No one can make you feel inferior without your consent." **Eleanor Roosevelt**

# The Quoted Life

122. "Always be yourself and have faith in yourself. Do not go out and look for a successful personality and try to duplicate it." **Bruce Lee**

123. "As soon as you trust yourself, you will know how to live." **Johann Wolfgang von Goethe**

124. "Always remember you are braver than you believe, stronger than you seem, and smarter than you think." **Christopher Robin**

125. "The moment you doubt whether you can fly, you cease forever to be able to do it." **J.M. Barrie**

126. "There is NOBODY like you, and once you realize that your entire future changes." **- Peter Voogd**

127. "You can't connect the dots looking forward; you can only connect them looking backward. So you have to trust that the dots will somehow connect in your future. You have to trust in something-- your gut, destiny, life, karma, whatever. This approach has never let me down, and it has made all the difference in my life." **Steve Jobs**

128. "Trust yourself. Create the kind of self that you will be happy to live with all your life. Make the most of yourself by fanning the tiny, inner sparks

of possibility into flames of achievement." **Golda Meir**

129. People will judge you regardless, so be what you want to be- **Peter Voogd**

130. "Confidence comes not from always being right but from not fearing to be wrong." **Peter T. Mcintyre**

131. "Be content to act, and leave the talking to others." **Baltasar**

132. "The moment you accept responsibility for EVERYTHING in your life is the moment you gain the power to change ANYTHING in your life." – **Hal Elrod**

133. "Argue for your limitations and, sure enough, they're yours." **Richard Bach**

134. "Nothing can stop the man with the right mental attitude from achieving his goal; nothing on earth can help the man with the wrong mental attitude." **Thomas Jefferson**

The Quoted Life

135. "Always be yourself and have faith in yourself. Do not go out and look for a successful personality and try to duplicate it." **Bruce Lee**

136. "Twenty years from now, you will be more disappointed by the things you didn't do than by the ones you did do. So throw off the bowlines. Sail away from the safe harbor. Catch the trade winds in your sail. Explore. Dream. Discover." **Mark Twain**

137. "The courage to be is the courage to accept oneself, in spite of being unacceptable." **Paul Tillich**

138. "Be more concerned with your character than your reputation, because your character is what you really are, while your reputation is merely what others think you are." -**John Wooden**

139. "To anyone that ever told you you're no good ... They're no better." **Hayley Williams**

140. "Insecurities will destroy you, while real confidence will take you to a level very few attain." - **Peter Voogd**

The Quoted Life

141. "Don't waste your energy trying to change opinions ... Do your thing, and don't care if they like it." **Tina Fey**

142. "Pride is holding your head up when everyone around you has theirs bowed. Courage is what makes you do it." **Bryce Courtenay**

143. "Until you value yourself, you won't value your time. Until you value your time, you won't do anything with it."- **Scott Peck**

144. It is never too late to be what you might have been. –**George Eliot**

145. "Trust yourself. You know more than you think you do." **Dr. Benjamin Spock**

146. "You yourself, as much as anyone in the entire universe, deserve your love and affection." **Buddha**

147. "You have no control over other people's taste, so focus on staying true to your own." **Tim Gunn**

The Quoted Life

148. "Don't wait until everything is just right. It will never be perfect. There will always be challenges, obstacles, and less than perfect conditions. So what? Get started now. With each step you take, you will grow stronger and stronger, more and more skilled, more and more self-confident, and more and more successful." **Mark Victor Hansen**

149. "It is not the mountain we conquer, but ourselves." **Sir Edmund Hillary**

150. "Optimism is the faith that leads to achievement. Nothing can be done without hope and confidence." **Helen Keller**

151. "If we all did the things we are capable of doing, we would literally astound ourselves." **Thomas Alva Edison**

152. "One important key to success is self-confidence. An important key to self-confidence is preparation." **Arthur Ashe**

153. To live a creative life, we must lose our fear of being wrong. ~**Anonymous**

The Quoted Life

154. "When you're different, sometimes you don't see the millions of people who accept you for what you are. All you notice is the person who doesn't." **Jodi Picoult**

155. "People are like stained-glass windows. They sparkle and shine when the sun is out, but when the darkness sets in their true beauty is revealed only if there is light from within." **Elisabeth Kübler-Ross**

156. "Once we believe in ourselves, we can risk curiosity, wonder, spontaneous delight, or any experience that reveals the human spirit." **E. E. Cummings**

157. "You can have anything you want if you are willing to give up the belief that you can't have it." **Dr. Robert Anthony**

158. "It is confidence in our bodies, minds, and spirits that allows us to keep looking for new adventures." **Oprah Winfrey**

159. "Shyness has a strange element of narcissism, a belief that how we look, how we perform, is truly important to other people." **Andre Dubus**

The Quoted Life

160. "You cannot be lonely if you like the person you're alone with." **Dr. Wayne Dyer**

161. "You wouldn't worry so much about what others think of you if you realized how seldom they do." **Eleanor Roosevelt**

162. "It's a dead-end street if you sit around waiting for someone else to tell you-you're OK." **Michael Pitt**

163. "Successful people have fear, successful people have doubts, and successful people have worries. They just don't let these feelings stop them." **T. Harv Eker**

164. "To double your net worth, double your self-worth. Because you will never exceed the height of your self-image." - **Robin Sharma**

IV. Quotes on the Importance of Continuous Learning:

165. "Learn to work harder on yourself than you do on your job. If you work hard on your job, you can make a living, but if you work hard on yourself you'll make a fortune." — **Jim Rohn**

166. "The best education you can get is investing in yourself, and that doesn't mean college or university."- **Warren Buffet**

167. The man who views the world at 50 the same as he did at 20 has wasted 30 years of his life." – **Muhammed Ali**

168. "Amateurs practice until they get it right; professionals practice until they can't get it wrong." - **Unknown**

169. "Ordinary people love entertainment. Extraordinary people adore education." - **Robin Sharma**

The Quoted Life

170. "Be patient with yourself. Self-growth is tender; it's holy ground. There's no greater investment." **Stephen Covey**

171. "Start taking your SELF to the next level so you can take your SUCCESS to the next level. It only happens in that order." - **Hal Elrod**

172. The difference between school and life? In school, you're taught a lesson and then given a test. In life, you're given a test that teaches you a lesson." –Tom Bodett Education costs money. But then so does ignorance. –**Sir Claus Moser**

173. Formal education will make you a living; self-education will make you a fortune." –**Jim Rohn**

174. Study as if you were going to live forever; live as if you were going to die tomorrow.- **Maria Mitchell**

175. "The less you 'think' you know, the greater your ability to learn and grow."- **Hal Elrod**

176. In order to learn the important lessons in life, one must, each day, surmount a fear." - **Ralph Waldo Emerson**

The Quoted Life

177. "There is a big difference between just learning something, and actually LIVING what you learn." **– Hal Elrod**

178. "There is no education like adversity." -**Disraeli**

179. "I have never let my schooling interfere with my education." -**Mark Twain**

180. To double your success, triple what you spend on personal development and professional learning. The person who knows the most becomes the best." **Anonymous**

181. He who is afraid to ask is ashamed of learning. ~ **Danish Proverb**

182. Live as if you were to die tomorrow. Learn as if you were to live forever." -**Mahatma Gandhi**

183. I have never let my schooling interfere with my education." -**Mark Twain**

V. Quotes on significance of Persistence:

184. "Many of life's failures are people who did not realize how close they were to success when they gave up." –**Thomas A. Edison**

185. "What seems to us as bitter trials are often blessings in disguise." **Oscar Wilde**

186. "Much of the stress that people feel doesn't come from having too much to do. It comes from not finishing what they've started." **David Allen**

187. "I hated every minute of training, but I said 'Don't quit. Suffer now and live the rest of your life as a champion." -**Muhammad Ali**

188. "Though no one can go back and make a brand new start, anyone can start from now and make a brand new ending." – **Carl Bard**

The Quoted Life

189. Be like a Postage Stamp- Stick to one thing, until you get there- **Josh Billings**

190. "Entrepreneurs average 3.8 failures before final success. What sets the successful ones apart is their amazing persistence." **Lisa M. Amos**

191. "When we are no longer able to change the situation, we are challenged to change ourselves." — **Victor Frankl**

192. "If you're going through hell, keep going." **Winston Churchill**

193. "You may have to fight a battle more than once to win it." **Margaret Thatcher**

194. "Many of life's failures are people who did not realize how close they were to success when they gave up." **Thomas A. Edison**

195. "You only live once, but if you do it right, once is enough." -**Mae West**

196. It takes 20 years to become an overnight success.– **Eddie Cantor**

The Quoted Life

197. Life has two rules: #1. Never quit #2. Always remember rule # 1." – **Unknown**

VI. **Quotes on Motivation:**

198. "Motivation is what gets you started. Habit is what keeps you going." **Jim Ryun**

199. People often say that motivation doesn't last. Well, neither does bathing. That's why we recommend it daily. –**Zig Ziglar**

200. "Make today the BEST day of your life, because there is no good reason not to." – **Hal Elrod**

201. Optimism is a happiness magnet. If you stay positive, good things and good people will be drawn to you. ~ **Mary Lou Retton**

202. Be miserable. Or motivate yourself. Whatever has to be done, it's always your choice. ~**Wayne Dyer**

The Quoted Life

203. "Motivation is a fire from within. If someone else tries to light that fire under you, chances are it will burn very briefly." -**Stephen Covey**

204. "The pessimist sees the difficulty in every opportunity. The optimist sees the opportunity in every difficulty." –**Winston Churchill**

205. "No extraordinary result ever came from the mediocre effort."- **Hal Elrod**

206. Motivation will almost always beat mere talent." — **Norman R. Augustin**

207. Your chances of success in any undertaking can always be measured by your belief in yourself." — **Robert Collier**

208. Motivation is a fire from within. If someone else tries to light that fire under you, chances are it will burn very briefly." -**Stephen Covey**

VII. Quotes on Happiness:

209. People are just as happy as they make up their minds to be." -**Abraham Lincoln**

210. "In the midst of movement and chaos, keep stillness inside of you." **Deepak Chopra**

211. "Happiness is not a station you arrive at, but a manner of traveling." **Margaret Lee Runbeck**

212. When one door of happiness closes, another opens, but often we look so long at the closed door that we do not see the one that has been opened for us. –**Helen Keller**

213. A man who dares to waste one hour of time has not discovered the value of life." –**Charles Darwin**

214. "Dream as if you'll live forever, live as if you'll die today." **James Dean**

The Quoted Life

215. "Doing what you like is freedom. Liking what you do is happiness." **Frank Tyger**

216. Learn how to be happy with what you have while you pursue all that you want.- **Jim Rohn**

217. "True happiness...arises, in the first place, from the enjoyment of one's self." **Joseph Addison**

218. "Tension is who you think you should be; relaxation is who you are." **Chinese Proverb**

219. "There is no stress in the world, only people thinking stressful thoughts and then acting on them." **Wayne Dyer**

220. "Happiness is a butterfly, which when pursued, is always beyond your grasp, but which, if you sit down quietly, may alight upon you." **Nathaniel Hawthorne**

221. "I've learned that people will forget what you said, people will forget what you did, but people will never forget how you made them feel." **Maya Angelou**

The Quoted Life

222. "Focus on the journey, not the destination. Joy is found not in finishing an activity but in doing it." **Greg Anderson**

223. "In our daily lives, we must see that it is not happiness that makes us grateful, but the gratefulness that makes us happy." **Albert Clarke**

****

Thank You!

Before you go, I would like to say thank you for purchasing and reading my book.

You could have picked amongst dozens of other books on this subject, but you took a chance and checked out this one.

So, big thanks for downloading this book and reading all the way to the end.

Now I'd like to ask for a small favor. **Could you please spend a minute or two and leave a review for this book on Amazon?**

Reviews are Gold to the Authors!

Your feedback will help me continue to write the kind of Kindle books that help you get results.

And if you loved it, please let me know.

The Quoted Life

Your Free Gift Bundle:

Did you download your Gift Bundle already?

Click and Download your Free Gift Bundle Below

Get Your Gift Bundle!

THREE KILLER BOOKS for FREE on:
1. Mind Hacking - in just 21 days!
2. Time Hacking- How to Cheat Time!
3. The Productivity Manifesto

&

TWO FREE VIDEOS to Understand Procrastinator's Mind and How to Use Procrastination for your Benefit

Click Here To GET INSTANT ACCESS

You can also grab your FREE GIFT BUNDLE through this below URL:

http://sombathla.com/freegiftbundle

About the Author

Som Bathla writes books that focus on changing old mindsets, overcoming self-defeating behavior & best strategies for enhancing the productivity and resourcefulness in all areas of life.

He has written more than half a dozen books on above subject and his many books have already touched the Amazon #1 Best Seller. He has good plans to continuously create more action guides to help readers to lead a productive and resourceful life (for details visit sombathla.com)

He is convinced about the limitlessness of the human potential and strongly believes that everyone has the potential of achieving more than one thinks about oneself. His life mantra is that a rewarding life is nothing but a series of small actions taken consistently on a daily basis with a positive and resourceful mindset.

Som resides in India where he spends most of his time reading, writing and enjoying time with his amazing wife and two sweet daughters. He is deeply committed to a path of

The Quoted Life

never-ending self-improvement and open to explore the best possibilities coming on his journey.

Made in the USA
Columbia, SC
18 October 2018